BOY SAYS

BOY SAYS (A BOOK WITH NO ENDING). Copyright © 2024 by Néstor Ponce and Max Ubelaker Andrade. This work carries a Creative Commons BY-NC-SA 4.0 International license, which means that you are free to copy and redistribute the material in any medium or format, and you may also remix, transform, and build upon the material, as long as you clearly attribute the work to the author (but not in a way that suggests the author or punctum books endorses you and your work), you do not use this work for commercial gain in any form whatsoever, and that for any remixing and transformation, you distribute your rebuild under the same license. http://creativecommons.org/licenses/by-nc-sa/4.0/

First edition published in 2024 by Uitgeverij
An imprint of punctum books, Earth, Milky Way
https://www.punctumbooks.com

ISBN-13: 978-1-68571-250-1 (print)
ISBN-13: 978-1-68571-251-8 (ePDF)
DOI: 10.53288/0528.1.00
LCCN: 2024946163
Library of Congress Cataloging Data is available from the Library of Congress

Editing: Vincent W.J. van Gerven Oei & SAJ
Book design: Vincent W.J. van Gerven Oei

This work has been published within the framework of the Sur Translation Support Programme of the Ministry of Foreign Affairs, International Trade and Worship of the Argentine Republic.

Obra editada en el marco del Programa Sur de Apoyo a las Traducciones del Ministerio de Relaciones Exteriores, Comercio Internacional y Culto de la República Argentina.

spontaneous acts of scholarly combustion

Programa **Sur**

NÉSTOR PONCE

boy says
(a book with no ending)

TRANSLATED BY MAX UBELAKER ANDRADE

⋮

Contents

Translator's Note	7
Giuseppe Ungaretti	12 · 13
Safo de Lesbos · Sappho of Lesbos	14 · 15
Florencia Pinar	16 · 17
N'dèye Coumba Mbengué Diakhaté	18 · 19
Juan Gelman	20 · 21
Sor Juana Inés de la Cruz	24 · 25
Jacinto Verdaguer	26 · 27
Discépolo	28 · 29
Rosario Castellanos	30 · 31
Juan Carlos Onetti	32 · 33
Federico Fellini	34 · 35
Alejandra Pizarnik	38 · 39
Nazim Hikmet	40 · 41
Alfonsina Storni	42 · 43
Fernando Pessoa	44 · 45
Louis Aragon	46 · 47
Álvaro Cunqueiro	50 · 51
Delmira Agustini	54 · 55
Silvina Ocampo	58 · 59

Dina Posada	60 · 61
John Keats	62 · 63
Jaime Gil de Biedma	66 · 67
Eugenio Montale	68 · 69
Proverbio swahili · Swahili Proverb	70 · 71
Mite Stefoski	72 · 73
Cesare Pavese	74 · 75
Octavio Paz	76 · 77
Milada Součková	78 · 79
Dulce María Loynaz	80 · 81
Anna Greki	82 · 83
Antonio Abad	86 · 87
Anne Hébert	88 · 89
Cecilia Meireles	90 · 91
Nicanor Parra	92 · 93
Tomas Tranströmer	94 · 95
Constantin Cavafy	96 · 97
Henri Michaux	100 · 101
Alejandro Pushkin · Alexander Pushkin	102 · 103
Keorapetse Kgositsile	104 · 105
Tomás Morales	106 · 107
Iryna Vikyrchak	108 · 109
Alfonso Gumucio Dagrón	110 · 111
Claudio Rodríguez Fer	112 · 113
Édouard Glissant	114 · 115

Translator's Note

The original title of this book is *Vos es*, an ungrammatical fragment that in English could be rendered as "You are"—though this erases the disjunction between the informal *voseo* and the conjugated verb. This gap has an important function. It gives the reader a chance to pause and read again, hearing the phonetic echo of another word. *Vos es* suddenly becomes *voces* (voices). Together, they create the conditions for the reader to hear, unexpectedly, a partially obscured idea—that you / are / voices.

How to respond to this suggestion is fully in the hands of the reader. As a translator, it was a useful reminder to consider how my voice (in this and other contexts) also belongs to others or carries others within it—how the voices that appear when I write or speak or think are reworked fragments, tones, styles, and rhythms, each holding traces of aversions, insights, ideologies, and ignorance.

Most of the poems in *Vos es* have the names of writers as their titles and it is tempting to read them as refashioned interpretations, as evocations or memories of the reading experience. Yet they are as marked by the author of the book as by the authors that they name; none of them make promises regarding their trustworthiness. Reading carefully, one can hear echoes across their pages: images and scents that repeat and connect, reminding us of the reader-writer (*vos*), while opening to a larger community that extends across time (*voces*). It is, together, a crowd, a chorus, or a personal library, which—once you read it—you also become part of.

The translation process of these poems always involved spending time with work of each named author. It is worth saying that these readings and re-readings are incomplete and partial. Some writers I knew well, others were new to me. At times, I found poetry, essays, or fiction that helped inform my choices—texts that provided clear reference points within the translations. Yet I suspect that the effects were also indirect, slight shifts in rhythm or style that did not fully register to me in the moment. I imagine that future readings will tug at the shape of these translations, bringing them into new dialogues and contexts.

Néstor Ponce has written that literature—that reading—has always invited him into a secret, invisible community, maintained by an ongoing dialogue between readers, texts, and authors that for him has extended across childhood, exile, and the violence of Argentina's military dictatorship. In this volume, a glimpse of this community emerges through the conversations between poems, writers, and texts, with repetitions that hint at a presence, an "author" who creates verses and brings them together for us to encounter and transform again.

If we momentarily rename all of these poems "Néstor Ponce," we can be brought back to the tenuous unity of the *vos* or the "boy" who speaks in multiple languages, tones, and identities—extending themselves, changing their shape, their form, without ever becoming fully, completely lost (without ever being fixed into a rigid maturity, an immutable identity). If we imagine these poems as a library, as part of our inner collection of books and voices, we can replace the poet's name with our own as we deepen our relationship with the authors it names.

By ending the book with a poem dedicated to Edouard Glissant, Ponce reminds us that these transformations are not inconsequential—that they can be the foundation for social, political, and spiritual possibilities, for new forms of justice, liberation, and love. Just as it might require a certain willingness to be shaped by the style and worldview of another person, the poetry that Ponce evokes through Glissant also refuses easy assimilation. It is happily contradictory, opaque, at ease with its unknowability, and unafraid of crossing boundaries without losing itself. As an ending poem, it calls out to the reader to break the rules, cross limits, and begin, again, to question their own unstable, growing library. Maybe it is a call to write.

Which is to say that if each poem is read as an invitation, we can never know what we are being invited to. There is risk there. A voice (composed of many voices) is not always easy to control or predict; it can alter the shape and reach of your own. Ponce suggests that only way forward is to leap, with confidence and abandon. Don't worry about what you might lose, he says: poetry is a thief but never steals.

Max Ubelaker Andrade

boy says

Giuseppe Ungaretti

En la vacía inmensidad de la ausencia
caben mares selvas y tréboles de diez hojas

Se pueden rascar las costras del tiempo
y alisar los callos del perjurio

Y como si esto no alcanzara
se abren las arrugas de la piedra en el agua

Giuseppe Ungaretti

In the open immensity of absence
there's room for oceans forests and ten-leaf clovers

You can scratch at the scabs of time
file down callouses of false witness

And as if this weren't enough
the wrinkles in the stone open up in the water

Safo de Lesbos

Señora infinita
me someto al arrullo
de tu viento que tirita
me acurruco
lleno de voces
en el campanario
de tu brusca boca

No queda tiempo
para la ciénaga del olvido
tampoco para la aurora
de dedos rosados

Viaja el carbón
hacia el alba imprevista
la sorpresa
de los pájaros remotos

Tu huella perdura
en la ausencia de mis manos

Sappho of Lesbos

Infinite lady
I submit to the nightsong
of your trembling wind
I curl up
filled with voices
in the bell tower
of your sudden mouth

No time
for the swamp of oblivion
nor for the dawn
rose-fingered

Soot travels
toward the unforeseen sunrise
the surprise
of distant birds

Your fingerprints persist
in the absence of my hands

Florencia Pinar

La tierra de las aves
es el cielo
o sea
un juramento
de hechizo y aire

que se hace verdor
y ráfagas
vientos eternos
como el vértigo del canto

Florencia Pinar

The land of the birds
is the sky
or rather
an oath
of witchcraft and air

that becomes greenness
and gusting
winds as eternal
as the vertigo of song

N'dèye Coumba Mbengué Diakhaté

El hilo de oro
une al contrabandista
con el filibustero
al bandido con el criminal

Rayo de oro
que va al puerto
al huerto de tu vientre

Lágrima de oro
por siempre reúne
al contrabandista
al ruin al genocida
que fue el fruto de un amor

N'dèye Coumba Mbengué Diakhaté

The golden thread
unites the smuggler
with the pirate
the bandit with the criminal

A golden ray
that goes to the port
to the orchard of your belly

A golden teardrop
forever bringing together
the smuggler
the miser the genocidal murderer
who flowered each from love

Juan Gelman

Ese poeta
llevaba un caballo fosforescente
que le cabalgaba los ojos
Desde algún rincón de la retina
se le caía la tristeza
en forma de vocales
era tan numerosa
que cobraba la forma de un tsunami
de intemperies perdidas

Las vocales se pegaban al alma
y con sus uñitas sucias
nos arrancaban las costras
y todos los silencios

Nunca vi un poeta
con tantos andamios en los hombros
cargaban botines de fútbol
un kilo de yerba
un barrilete de bandoneones

Uno se lleva la infancia
atada con un piolín al cuerpo
Los años caracolean
como jaurías perros callejeros
ladran versos de muchedumbre
esquinas con almacén
o pelotas de cuero

Juan Gelman

That poet
carried a phosphorescent horse
that rode his eyes
From some corner of a retina
the sadness fell
in the form of vowels
so vast
it formed a tsunami
of lost and open skies

The vowels clung to the soul
and their little dirty fingernails
tore off our scabs
and all the silences

I never saw a poet
with so much scaffolding on their shoulders
it carried soccer cleats
a kilo of máte
a barrel of bandoneons

One carries childhood
tied by twine to the body
The years encircle
like hounds street dogs
that bark crowd verses
corners with little shops
or balls of leather

Nunca conversé con un poeta
tan lleno de silencios
la irreverencia
se le caía a puñados de los labios
y le servía
para arañar la luz

Un domingo lluvioso
me lo encontré
a las doce
en la puerta de mi casa
duerma usté ciudadano
sin la conciencia tranquila
por supuesto
y pórtese mal
me dijo voluntarioso
mientras los escuerzos
escarchan los deseos

Llevaba un abrigo gris
fumaba un particulares sin filtro
que ya no se fabrican:
vengo de otro lugar
confesó
arrugando la lengua

soy poeta
y se fue
rastrillando la noche
con sus pasos
llenos de versos insomnes

I never spoke with a poet
so full of silences
the irreverence
fell in fistfuls from his lips
and he used it
to tangle up the light

One rainy Sunday
I found him
at twelve
by the door of my house
sleep, my deares' citizen
without of course
a clean conscience
behave badly
he said with confidence
while the horned frogs
frost over desires

He wore a gray coat
smoked a filterless particulares
that no one makes anymore:
i'm from somewhere else
he confessed
wrinkling his tongue

i am a poet
and he left
raking the night
with his footsteps
of insomniac verses

Sor Juana Inés de la Cruz

Los miedos infantiles
eran de pozo y túnel
nunca aprendí otro horror
más elocuente
del que salía de tus olvidos

En vez del catecismo
ella prefería los saltos hondos
medio infinitos
según ciertos testigos
no del todo recomendables

Eran trapecios
no había redes o escaleras
estrategias
para quemar los huesos
iluminada por los fogonazos
de los proyectores del circo

Y seguía el vacío
            vacío
                      en su oquedad
                                      interminable

Sor Juana Inés de la Cruz

The childhood fears
were made of well and tunnel
I never knew a horror
more eloquent
than what escaped your omissions

Instead of catechism
she preferred leaping into depths
nearly infinite
according to certain
not entirely trustworthy witnesses

They were trapezes
without nets or stairs
strategies
for burning bones
illuminated by the flashing
of circus lights

And she would follow the emptiness
        empty
                in its hollowness
                          with no end

Jacinto Verdaguer

Se huele el aliento que sopla
los vapores de la tierra
que recorre valles y montañas
alzando el grito ronco
hasta la sordera fina de las playas
hasta los surcos como labios
sangrientos de las viñas
hasta los bosques cubiertos de piñas

Catalunya

Jacinto Verdaguer

You can smell the breath that blows
the vapors of the earth
that crosses valleys and mountains
raising the hoarse cry
to the smoothed deafness of the beaches
to the vineyard furrows
bloodied like lips
to forests blanketed in pinecones

Catalunya

Discépolo

El cantor silabeó
que la lucha es cruel
y es mucha
que se hace de anocheceres
salpicando naufragios
en el río de la plata

Yo siempre quise ser un surubí
para bailar tangos tornasolados
entre el dos x cuatro de tus piernas

Tener una lucha
entre tus brazos
que fuera larga y mucha
como un amanecer
de revoltijos entre las sábanas

Cuando fui por fin una vigilia
entre tus olores y humedades
el techo se iba alejando
se separaba de tu piel
nos miraba lleno de envidia

Discépolo

The singer pronounced
that the struggle's too long
too far gone
and made of nightfalls
splashing shipwrecks
in the silver-plated river

I always tried to be a sorubim catfish
to dance spinning tangos
within the two x four of your legs

To struggle
in your arms
may it be too long too far gone
like waking in
twisted sheets

Finally fast awake
among your smells your sweat
the ceiling began to float away
separating itself from your skin
to watch us full of envy

Rosario Castellanos

Un danzón
haciendo roscas de días
y en la flor del labio
un fundamento

Tuviste entre los brazos
fosforescencias de pájaras
que revoloteaban por encima
de tormentas coaguladas
y picoteaban
la brisa del amanecer

Por vegetales sedientos
corría el suspiro
del viejo polvo enamorado

Crecía el eco de los pañuelos
inertes en la noche densa
Palpitaban los conejos
Corría el suspiro
apretado en el gemido de tu boca

Rosario Castellanos

A *danzón*
turning days into spirals
and in the flower of the lip
a foundation

You had in your arms
phosphorescenses of hens
that fluttered above
coagulated storms
and pecked
at the morning wind

Through thirsty vegetables
raced the sigh
of old and enamored dust

The echo of still handkerchiefs
grew in the density of night
The rabbits shook
The sigh raced
held tight in the cry of your mouth

Juan Carlos Onetti

Siempre hubo otros miedos
de pozo y leche negra
vahos de telarañas lentas
y una ciudad que arde
tal crepúsculo que quema
los recuerdos

Fueron rutas de vidrios quebrados
con ecos de pasos distantes
transpirando cuervos
y otros fragmentos de polvo

Cierta noche perdida
se dijo:
toda mi vida fui pichón
de cabeza salpicada de rocío
burlón ante las amenazas
de los oscuros del mundo

Juan Carlos Onetti

There were always other fears
of wells and black milk
vapors of slow spiderweb
and a city on fire
that dusk that burns
memories

They were paths of broken glass
with echoes of distant steps
sweating out ravens
and other fragments of dust

One lost night
he said to himself:
all my life I was a pigeon
its head flecked with dew
laughing at the threats
of the darkest ones of the world

Federico Fellini

Nunca estuve en Rímini
y otros soles pintan
mi cabeza cana
¿Por qué caminos
me perdí / oscuro
antes de llegar a Rímini?
¿Qué arenas locas
qué calles de penumbra
luces como pocas
recorrió Federico?

Nunca fui a Rímini
Nunca fui

Hay brisas ardientes
enroscadas en el cielo
por verduras y yodo
por gritos y ansiedades

Nunca fui a Rímini
Nunca fui

Sueño recorridos
en el amanecer
cuando las vacías calles
se despiertan
y encontrarte

Federico Fellini

I was never in Rimini
and other suns paint
my whitened hair
On what roads
did I lose myself / dark
before coming to Rimini?
What wild sands
what shadowed streets
lights unmatched
did Federico wander?

Never did I go to Rimini
Never did I go

There are scalding breezes
curled in the sky
for greens and iodine
for shouts and worries.

Never did I go to Rimini
Never did I go

I dream of walks
at daybreak
when the empty streets
wake up
and of finding you

abandonado
con un cigarrillo
colgando de los labios

Nunca fui a Rímini

abandoned
with a cigarette
hanging from your lips

Never did I go to Rimini

Alejandra Pizarnik

De tan triste tu reflejo
el espejo se fue solo
por el amargor del adiós

Fue el lugar de la infancia
un primer beso
las manchas mojando el hombro

Gotas secas
cayendo en la piedra
horadando
el fin de un atisbo

No quedan horizonte
ni brumas cómplices
ni abismo

No hay tiempo
el tiempo es hoy

Alejandra Pizarnik

Your reflection was so sad
that the mirror left alone
without the bitterness of a goodbye

It was the place of childhood
a first kiss
the shoulder stained wet

Dry drops
falling on the stone
drilling
the end of a faint light

There's no more horizon
no conspiratorial fog
no abyss

There's no time
the time is today

Nazim Hikmet

Fulano y Mengano
vienen del árabe
Fulān y Man kān
o sea formas ávidas
de darle caras al silencio
para que todo nombre
sea pronunciado
al fin de cuentas

Nazim Hikmet

Fulano and Mengano
come from the Arabic
Fulān and Man kān
avid ways I think
of lending faces to silence
so that every name
might be pronounced
before the story is over

Alfonsina Storni

En el páramo ardiente
o cayendo
en la ávida ciénaga
siempre existen
proyectos del mal
o páginas de olvidarte

Tu nombre aguarda acurrucado
listo para erguirse y saltar
como un antorcha de sal
que me empuña por las pestañas
y me lleva al sol

La ceguera radiante
gira tornasolada
es la brújula
que me ancla en el mar

Alfonsina Storni

On the scorched plains
or falling
in eager swamps
there are always
evil designs
or pages to forget you

Your name is curled up and waiting
ready to stand and jump
like a salt torch
that grips me by the eyelashes
and carries me to the sun

Radiant blindness
twirls iridescent
it is the compass
that anchors me in the sea

Fernando Pessoa

El silencio
dice más que la palabra
su hueco cobija
el deseo del beso
el milagro de la dicha

No digas nada no
no es necesario
el silencio habla
trae el tiempo
la niebla del ayer
el desvelo de tu boca

Fernando Pessoa

Silence
says more than the word
its hollow covers
the kiss's desire
the miracle of joy

No don't say anything no
no need
silence speaks
it brings time
yesterday's fog
the revelation of your mouth

Louis Aragon

Los ojos de mi mujer son de menta y miel
don Luis
Una mañana vi desenroscarse en sus niñas
una multitud de yeguas enfurecidas
Iban pidiendo piedad
los animales
enroscaban sus colas húmedas
a la furia escarlata del amanecer
Mi mujer pestañeaba indolente
y la secuencia siguiente
era un andamio de faroles fosforescentes
que caían en la bahía de Río de Janeiro
La diosa Yemanjá se ponía celosa
y no era para menos
porque los iris de menta y miel
empañaban todos los solsticios

Otra vez en un cine
me colé en sus pupilas
y anduve navegando intrépido
entre huracanes y torbellinos
y me desperté en una cresta de espuma
con la espada del capitán

Los ojos de mi mujer
don Luis
son de menta y miel

Louis Aragon

My lady's eyes are mint and honey
don Luis
One morning in her pupils I saw unfurl
a multitude of furious mares
They were asking for mercy
the animals
curled their damp tails
at the scarlet fury of the dawn
My lady blinked indifferent
and the sequence that followed
was a scaffold of phosphorescent lanterns
falling in the bay of Rio de Janeiro
The goddess Iemanjá became jealous
and it was no wonder
because her irises of mint and honey
clouded every solstice

Another time in a theater
I fell through her pupils
and navigated intrepidly forward
through hurricanes and whirlwinds
and awoke on a crest of sea foam
with the captain's sword

The eyes of my lady
don Luis
are mint and honey

y con ellos
atravieso
todas las montañas
y descubro
lo que respira por detrás

and with them
I cross
every mountain
and discover
all that breathes beyond

Álvaro Cunqueiro

Cuando fallece un hombre
todos los días
ruge la travesía
de la vida
tal un niño llorando

Se mueren entonces
las calles de La Plata
los sueños náufragos
se quedan sin aliento
los caballos patean
adoquines canallas

Se callan

La muerte se lleva cabalgatas
voces llenas de instantes
el pasto bajo los botines

Se queda sin aliento

Se trepa a las estrellas
y no va solo
arrastra a la ciudad
a los amigos
a las entrañas
con un coro de botellas

Álvaro Cunqueiro

When a man perishes
every day
life's journey
roars
like a crying child

They die then
the streets of La Plata
the shipwrecked dreams
left breathless
horses kick
bastard cobblestones

They become quiet

Death makes off with processions
voices full of instants
grass under boots

It's left breathless

It crawls up to the stars
and it doesn't go alone
it carries the city
the friends
the entrails
with a chorus of bottles

No va solo
el hombre
que muere cada día

He doesn't go alone
the man
who dies every day

Delmira Agustini

Te inclinabas hacia mí
suave y tan palpable
como una rosca de músculos
abiertos para mi carne
bailabas un hervor de espuma
en mi pecho
y caías inexorable y caías

Las cortas noches
y los aciagos días
corrían inexorables y corrían
y yo tanteaba la oscuridad
a la espera de sus luces
y del sauce de tu melancolía

Volabas sobre mi volabas
como una garza un águila
una pluma de promesas
que flota en el firmamento
y abre el crepúsculo

Te esperé una madrugada
envuelta en lirios
decidida a separar tus párpados
y descubrir el secreto del horizonte

Delmira Agustini

You would bow toward me
soft and so palpable
like a spiral of muscles
open for my flesh
dance a roiling foam
within my chest
and fall unyielding and fall

Short nights
and cursed days
ran unyielding and ran
and I reached out to the darkness
waiting for its lights
and the willow of your melancholy

You would fly over me you would fly
like a heron an eagle
a feather of promises
that floats in the firmament
and opens the dawn

I waited for you one morning
covered in irises
determined to open your eyelids
and discover the horizon's secret

Te echaste atrás
y te envolviste en un pliegue
y te perdiste por un
inexorable hueco de la sombra
inexorable

You flung yourself back
you wrapped yourself up in a fold
and were lost in an
unyielding hole in the shadow
unyielding

Silvina Ocampo

En algún recinto azul de la patria
laten escondidos atardeceres
se arman con miradas lentas
que atraviesan el tiempo
y las ruedas de las carretas

Cuántas noches no habré oído
los suspiros vagos
huyendo en la desmesura
como cristales rotos
en la palma de la mano

Campos de esquinas rosadas
y almacenes con rejas
habitados con milongas
arpegios y facones

Planicies de las que se yerguen
urbes a los saltos
y que vuelven a caer
en la monotonía de los pajonales

Silvina Ocampo

In some blue corner of the nation
beat hidden away evenings
they are armed with slow looks
traveling across time
and the wheels of carts

How many nights will I not have heard
indistinct sighs
fleeing in excess
like wineglass shards
in the palm of one's hand

Landscapes of pink corners
and gated grocery stores
inhabited by milongas
arpeggios and long knives

Plains from which rise
leaping cities
that fall once more
in the monotony of the scrublands

Dina Posada

Fue una noche rumorosa
hecha de sábanas plegadas
y almohadas en el aire
un piececito temblaba
como un gorrión de luz
entre las piernas

Fue una noche de quejidos
pintando líneas ondulantes
que iban del techo
a las entrañas
de la perplejidad
al grito

Fue una noche como tantas
fue una noche como pocas
y el temblor que hoy provoca

Sigue tensando el aliento

Dina Posada

It was a night of murmurs
made of folded sheets
and pillows in the air
a little foot trembled
like a sparrow of light
between one's legs

It was a night of moaning
painting undulating lines
that went from the roof
to the entrails
from confusion
to the cry

It was a night like so many
it was a night like none other
and today the trembling it invites

Still tightens the breath

John Keats

Los ruiseñores son imborrables
son perplejos
atraviesan calendarios y planetas
y su trino resuena
en el cuenco de las manos
de reyes y labriegos
En inglés ruiseñor
se dice
nightingale
que es un arpegio movedizo
que suena a rossignol
o a ruiseñor
e incluso a usignolo

Cuando el poeta
los oye cantar
hace trinos con los dedos
se le llenan los dedos
de trinos
los dedos se rellenan
de ruiseñores
que hablan en inglés
en italiano o en guaraní
se ponen a zumbar
sobre los hombros
trazan corcheas entre los olivos
y se quedan para siempre

John Keats

The nightingales are indelible
perplexed
they travel across calendars and planets
and their song echoes
in the bowl of the hands
of kings and laborers
In Spanish nightingale
is pronounced
ruiseñor
which is a shifting arpeggio
that sounds like rossignol
or nightingale
and even usignolo

When the poet
hears them singing
he makes his fingers trill
his fingers are filled
with birdsong
the fingers are refilled
with nightingales
that speak Spanish
Italian or Guaraní
they begin to buzz
over the shoulders
tracing quavers between the olive trees
and remain forever

en la misma rama
en el mismo verso

on the same branch
on the same verse

Jaime Gil de Biedma

Tus dedos acarician
los surcos de la arena
peinan un susurro insistente
abierto de cicatrices

Siempre amé los bares despojados
la inclemencia de ramblas vacías
los desvelos de lobos extraviados

Tus dedos trabajan
la escarcha de la memoria
amasan su pulpa
secan sus lágrimas

Siempre amé las estrategias de ceniza
los perros vagabundos
y los rugidos de leonas ausentes

Tus dedos suavizan
lo intangible
bañan de sed las tormentas
se acuestan con la bruma
y me bañan la eternidad

Jaime Gil de Biedma

Your fingers caress
furrows of sand
comb an insistent whisper
open to healed skin

I always loved abandoned bars
the harshness of empty boulevards
the sleeplessness of errant wolves

Your fingers work
the frost of memory
knead its flesh
dry its tears

I always loved the strategies of ash
vagabond dogs
and the roars of absent lionesses

Your fingers smooth
what cannot be touched
bathe storms with thirst
lie down within the fog
and for me they bathe eternity

Eugenio Montale

Amanece de nuevo
lo presiento
restaña la claridad
las heridas nocturnas
en las paredes

Nada se mueve
todo es ausencia de aromas
el sendero el techo los muebles sordos

Mi cuerpo
extendido insensible de partida

¿Amanece o es el fin?

Eugenio Montale

It's dawn again
I sense it
clarity staunches
the nocturnal wounds
on the walls

Nothing moves
everything is an absence of scents
the path the roof the deaf furniture

My body
extended unfeeling from the beginning

It is the dawn or is it over?

Proverbio swahili

Una tarde húmeda
me encogí en sus ubres

Pequeño como libélula
ardiente como savia

Mariposas volaban
serpentinas del aire

Tormentas me hirieron
voces me retorcieron

La palabra caía
como brecha encendida

Swahili Proverb

One humid afternoon
I sank into its udders

Small as a dragonfly
shining like sap

Butterflies were flying
streamers in the air

Storms wounded me
voices contorted me

The word was falling
like an ignited breach

Mite Stefoski

La prensa nunca publica
noticias desconcertantes:

las islas del Caribe
están envueltas en papel celofán morado
la cruz del sur
gira locamente sobre su eje
los tranvías avanzan a los saltos
un ciprés
creció al revés

La televisión
no le va en zaga:

las avutardas jamás graznan
variaciones de Beethoven
unas hormigas coloradas fabrican
arquitecturas de azúcar y miel
los murciélagos se besan
y les sangran los ojos enamorados

No habría que despertar
nunca / jamás
never / jamais
a la rutina
del previsible mundo

Mite Stefoski

The press never publishes
disconcerting news:

the islands of the Caribbean
are covered in purple cellophane
the southern cross
spins wildly on its axis
trains leap forward
a cypress
grew backwards

The television
is not far behind:

the great bustards never squawk
Beethoven variations
some fire ants construct
architectures of sugar and honey
bats kiss
and their enamored eyes bleed

One should not wake
never / jamais
nunca / jamás
the routine
of the foreseeable world

Cesare Pavese

¿Eran rojos, fueron azules, serán negros todavía?
A veces los olvido
me arrullo en lianas
escurridizas interminables

Busco su color, interrogo sus formas ocultas

A veces los recuerdo
pero cambian
se hacen fulminantes
se deshacen y crepitan
otras lloran y se enternecen

¿O son de menta y miel
y será la muerte
y será tu compañía?

Cesare Pavese

Were they red, were they blue, black will they still be?
I forget them sometimes
and sing myself lullabies in vines
slippery interminable

I look for their color, interrogate their hidden forms

Sometimes I remember them
but they change
become evasive
they fall apart and crackle
others cry and are moved

Or are they made of mint and honey
and will it be death
and will it be your company?

Octavio Paz

Doradas curvas
al sur hasta la grupa
de vello azul

Octavio Paz

To the south
golden curves
until the haunches of blue curls

Milada Soucková

El amanecer de Praga
se revuelve
cruje
se desmenuza
entre la pereza de crestas grises
y picos lentos de nieve

Corre en las láminas del ferrocarril
en el empedrado del barrio antiguo
y se precipita hacia el Moldava

Viaja en la corriente
se revuelca en el frío
renace
se hace
en el cielo azul

Milada Soucková

Dawn in Prague
turns
cracks
crumbles
in the laziness of gray crests
and the slow peaks of snow

It runs through train track blades
in the cobblestones of the old quarter
and rushes toward the Moldova

It travels in the currents
rolls around in the cold
it is reborn
remade
in the blue of the sky

Dulce María Loynaz

¿Cuáles son los recuerdos
del viejo espejo desconchado?
¿Cuántas lágrimas reflejó su brillo
qué amarguras su dolor?

Pasaron por sus nervios cristalinos
las sonrisas los perfumes
las distancias y los días
los arrebatos de una noche
las agonías de las tías solteronas

¿Qué colores tendrá de mí?
¿Qué arabescos de mi talle?

Hasta que el peso de tanto tiempo
lo derrumbe
y se marche con nosotros
perdido en las estrías

Dulce María Loynaz

What are those memories
of the old chipped mirror?
How many tears did its shine reflect
how much bitterness its pain?

Through its crystalline nerves traveled
the smiles the perfumes
the distances and the days
the fits of a night
the deaths of unmarried aunts

Which of my colors does it hold?
Which arabesques of my form?

Until the weight of so much time
breaks it down
and it leaves with us
lost in the striations

Anna Greki

Todos dormimos una noche
en una ciudad de casas suspendidas
albas como la tiza /
de muros tibios
penetrados por la brisa

Soñamos mientras
se desprendían las casas
rodando como terrones de azúcar
y salpicaban el mar
que las recibía gorgojeando
como una gaviota hambrienta
en el grumo de la claridad

Todos una vez
nos apretamos en los lechos
en tanto crepitaba el fuego
de las astillas nocturnas
y por los techos reptaban
halcones harapientos

En tanto / al mismo tiempo
seguían tumbándose
las paredes de labios de espuma
le hablaban a la noche
frases de otras tierras
se precipitaban hacia el tiempo

Anna Greki

We all slept one night
in a city of suspended houses
dawns like chalk /
lukewarm walls
penetrated by the wind

We dreamt while
the houses fell away
rolling like sugar cubes
and splashed into the sea
which received them gurgling
like a hungry gull
in the coagulation of clarity

We all one time
held each under the covers
while the fire gave off sparks
from nocturnal wood chips
and across the roofs crept
vagabond falcons

Meanwhile / simultaneously
they kept crashing down
the walls of foam lips
they spoke to the night
sentences from other lands
falling toward time

como una paloma
transida de cáscaras de huevo

Mañana será mañana
mañana será otro día
el vértigo del futuro
el qué hacer

Y con la luz
se abría el canto
llameante
del sol

like a dove
tormented by eggshells

Tomorrow will be tomorrow
tomorrow will be another day
the vertigo of the future
the every day work

And with the light
the song opened
in the fire
of the sun

Antonio Abad

Revoloteó en el lecho
como una flor
de pétalos encendidos

Se volcó en mi boca
se derramó en mi seno

Caí en un hueco
de sueños insensatos

Me llevó por encima
de sábanas sudorosas

Y volé, volé
como un jadeo
absorto de luz

Antonio Abad

She twisted in bed
like a flower
with lit petals

Leapt in my mouth
melted on my breast

I fell in a hole
of senseless dreams

She carried me above
the sweaty bedsheets

And I flew, I flew
like a gasp
filled with light

Anne Hébert

Nada más abismal
que la pena de un niño
en un prado

Llanto que se acuesta
en la breve tarde
mientras acecha la nevada

Lágrimas que se hielan
en la hierba dura
Lágrimas que vuelan
y se hacen rocío
para verter
la más honda
tristeza del mundo

Anne Hébert

Nothing more vast
than the sorrow of a child
on a field

A cry that lays down
in the short afternoon
while the snow lies in wait

Tears that freeze
in the stiff grass
Tears that fly
and become dew
so as to release
the deepest
sadness of the world

Cecilia Meireles

Ando con una saudade encima
que no me la quita
ni un carnaval de tucanes

Se me pega en los hombros
y me susurra nombres ausentes
tiempo que fue y será:
aquella revolución de besos perdidos
fernando corriendo desorbitado
delia cayendo de la cornisa
una multitud herida
desbocando sueños

Despegan los aviones de Niterói
se pierden en las nubes
en el qué será
de latitudes extrañas y revueltas

Nos dejan la saudade
salpicando llantos
encuentros ávidos
promesas del calendario

Cecilia Meireles

I walk with a *saudade*
that can't be lifted
not even by a toucan carnival

It's bound to my shoulders
and whispers absent names
time that was and will be:
that revolution of lost kisses
fernando spinning out of orbit
delia falling off the ledge
a wounded crowd
tearing off dreams

The planes take off from Niterói
disappear in the clouds
in the what will be
of strange and twisted latitudes

They leave us the *saudade*
splashing cries
eager meetings
calendar promises

Nicanor Parra

Yo tengo dos ojos (igualitos)
vos una sola mano
qué hacemos
con esta anatomía
con esta dicha
que se completa
tanto

Nicanor Parra

I have two eyes (and they're identical)
you one hand only
what should we do
with this anatomy
with this good fortune
that is made whole
so often

Tomas Tranströmer

La frontera es la bruma
los copos de nieve
las capas de nieve
sobre los pinares
los olvidos entre la piel
y los guantes

El desierto que se quema
entre los labios y el beso
la distancia
desde tu pecho
al olvido

La frontera se hizo
para ser rota y rebasada
para vivir
en el atropello del deseo
con una copa ambarina
junto a la chimenea

Tomas Tranströmer

The border is the fog
the snowflakes
the snow peaks
on the pines
all that's forgotten between skin
and gloves

The desert that burns
between the lips and the kiss
the distance
from your chest
to forgetting

The border was made
to be broken and left behind
to live
in the accidents of desire
with an amber glass
by the chimney

Constantin Cavafy

En cualquier instante
desde la dicha o las colinas
desde la tempestad o las dunas
llegan los Bárbaros

El trueno de los cascos
el ronco aullido de los carros
va rompiendo el horizonte
estrella cruces y estatuas de piedad

Se han muerto los dioses
ardieron los templos de la fe
cayeron cruces de malta
manos tejidas con fibras de seda
músicas apretadas como plegarias

Desde hace siglos
cabalgan los Bárbaros
las patrias infinitas

Nuestros gobernantes los aguardan
con las llaves de las ciudades
el raso de las alcobas
el gemido que se escapa
les ofrendan sus mujeres

Constantin Cavafy

At any instant
from happiness or the hills
from the storm or the dunes
come the Barbarians

The thunder of helmets
the hoarse scream of the carts
breaks the horizon
destroys crosses and pious statues

The gods have died
they burned the temples of the faith
all the Maltese crosses fell
hands woven with silk threads
songs as tight as prayers

For centuries now
the Barbarians ride
across infinite countries

Our leaders wait for them
with the keys to the cities
the bedroom satin
the escaped whimper
they offer up their women

Yo siempre me opuse a la barbarie
me degollaron en Pekín
en un campo de látigos yertos
caí en las afueras de Amsterdam
en un campo de tulipanes abiertos
y una madrugada me levanté
adulado en un museo
alzando espadas que nunca imaginé

Y /
como los Bárbaros
resucito

I was always opposed to barbarity
they cut my throat in Beijing
on a field of rigid whips
in the outskirts of Amsterdam I fell
upon a field of open tulips
and one morning I got up
was worshipped in a museum
raising swords that I had never imagined

And /
like the Barbarians
I am resurrected

Henri Michaux

¿A quién se le ocurrió encerrar a los Zapallos? Cuando es sabido que no toleran el roce de las bolsas de arpillera, las ecuaciones de más de diez dígitos o las canciones de cuna desafinadas? El desconcertado victimario produjo más de un accidente con tan poca calculada actitud: grupos de Zapallos ocuparon estaciones de ferry en parajes tan diversos como Colón, Santa Bárbara, Jersey o Rade de Saint-Michel; otros—no menos pertinentes—se dedicaron a organizar conciertos soplando en papel de celofán, acompañados por alas de abejas y gruñidos de toros en celo. La amenaza fue terrible y los gobernantes promovieron medidas anti-Zapallos. Ignorantes: cuando un Zapallo se larga a galopar bajo cielo abierto, nada ni nadie dejará de sonreír. De hecho, las arpilleras fueron carcomidas por el desdén y la vergüenza y hoy en día ya no es tan extraño toparse con un Zapallo leyendo en tu cama a poetas surrealistas belgas o buscando en un huerto frutos tropicales en pleno invierno. Pero esa es otra historia.

Henri Michaux

Whose idea was is to lock up the Squash? Especially since it's widely known that that they don't respond well to burlap sacks, equations exceeding ten digits, or out-of-tune lullabies? The disconcerted killer's poorly calibrated calculations produced more than few accidents: groups of Squash occupied ferry landings in locations as far-flung as Colón, Santa Bárbara, Jersey, or Rade de Saint-Michel; others—no less important—dedicated themselves to organizing concerts blowing on cellophane, accompanied by the wings of bees and the grunts of bulls in heat. The threat was terrible and government officials proposed anti-Squash measures. Ignoramuses: when a Squash goes off galloping under the open sky, nothing and no one can sidestep a smile. In fact, the burlap was eaten up by shame and disdain and today it's not even that strange to encounter a Squash reading Belgian surrealist poets in your bed or searching in a garden for tropical fruits in the wintertime. But that's another story.

Alejandro Pushkin

¿Quién podrá amarte como yo
en silencio y temblor de párpados?
¿Quién esculpiendo montañas
y deshojando pétalos de nubes?

En las calles quebradas
en las grietas de la brisa
bajo lunas de cartón
y tardes enloquecidas de saliva

Y yo
tan discreto
ardiendo de brasas
quemado
en mi propia letra

Alexander Pushkin

Who could love you as I do
silently with eyelids trembling?
Who sculpting mountains
and plucking petals from clouds?

In the broken streets
in the cracks of the wind
under moons made of cardboard
and spit-crazed evenings

And I
so discreet
seething in embers
burning
in my own script

Keorapetse Kgositsile

Cuidado hijo mío
venimos de un mismo
carnaval confuso
mundo sin piedad ni medida
tierra de pantanos hondos
de olores sin memoria

Siempre he ido
en busca de voces quebradas
he nadado a la deriva
de aguas tapizadas de estrellas

Por eso cuidado hijo mío
carne de mi carne
sal de mi sed
cornisa de mis labios
busquemos juntos
la vendimia del deseo

Keorapetse Kgositsile

Careful my child
we come from the same
confused carnival
world without pity or measure
land of deep marshes
of scents without memory

I have always gone
searching for broken voices
I have swum adrift
in star-carpeted waters

And so careful my child
flesh of my flesh
salt of my thirst
cornice of my lips
we shall seek together
the harvest grapes of desire

Tomás Morales

Recorro el pétalo de espuma
con la ciega ilusión de hacerte mía
atravieso el sueño de las porfías
en la suave pelambre de tu bruma

No hay olvido
todo es hoy

Tomás Morales

I see the shape of the foam petal
and wish stupidly that I were yours
I traverse labors that dreams obscure
in the soft pelt your fog has settled

There is no oblivion
all is now

Iryna Vikyrchak

Caigas donde caigas
habrá siempre un trozo de cielo
un ramillete de nubes
algún sol desmadejando la grisura

Cuando caigas
habrá siempre un silencio de buey
acompañando un grito
y también un coro de réquiem
en el estrépito de la noche

Al caer
el túnel abrirá sus fauces
hechas de vacíos y navajas
Tu cuerpo será tu cuerpo
tu recuerdo en las pupilas

Iryna Vikyrchak

Fall where you may
there will always be a piece of sky
a bouquet of clouds
some sun loosening the gray

When you fall
there will always be an ox's silence
accompanied by a scream
and also a requiem chorus
in the racket of the night

Falling
the tunnel will open up its maw
made of blades and emptinesses
Your body will be your body
your memory in the pupils

Alfonso Gumucio Dagrón

¿Qué es tu olor?
¿Un esplendor de menta y miel
que se acuesta en el ocaso?
¿Qué es tu boca?
¿El lugar de todas las palabras
y la única saliva?
¿Qué son tus pies?
¿Un vibrar de frutillas
que me llenan los silencios?
¿Qué es qué es?
¿Preguntas y preguntas
que se graban en la piel?
Para siempre

Alfonso Gumucio Dagrón

What is your scent?
A mint and honey splendor
that lays down in the sunset?
What is your mouth?
The place of every word
and the essential saliva?
What are your feet?
A vibration of strawberries
that fill up my silences?
What is what is?
Questions and questions
engraved on skin?
Forever

Claudio Rodríguez Fer

Él
que tantos hombres fue
se encontró una vez
con los simulacros las voces
los olores los perjurios
de la infancia

Él
se preguntó
cómo fue una vida
en el mar de la ignorancia

Soltó un do de pecho
y se subió
a los caballos azules de Galicia

Claudio Rodríguez Fer

He
who was so many men
once found himself
faced with the simulacra the voices
the scents the perjuries
of childhood

He
asked himself
how a life was lived
in the sea of ignorance

And let loose a *do* from his chest
before climbing
on the blue horses of Galicia

Édouard Glissant

La poesía es ladrona
pero no roba
se apropia de las palabras
las desnuda
las abre a las calles

La poesía masca el odio
anega el amor
es contradictoria
tiene manos suaves
de iracundo pelaje

La poesía es equina
anda con dos patas rengas
tiene belfo humeante
y grupa de puntos cardinales

La poesía es omnívora
y no descartable
posee nueve costillas
y fecunda con rara facilidad

La poesía es bicéfala
con una lengua lame la incertidumbre
con la otra restaña misterios
con otra escondida
revela piedras de cuarzo

Édouard Glissant

Poetry's a thief
but never steals
it appropriates words
takes off their clothes
opens them to the street

Poetry chews up hate
inundates love
it's contradictory
has soft hands
of irascible fur

Poetry is equine
walks with two lame legs
has a smoking lip
and cardinal point haunches

Poetry is omnivorous
can't be discarded
possesses nine ribs
and fertilizes with rare ease

Poetry is bicephalous
with one tongue it laps uncertainty
with the other it staunches mysteries
and with another one, hidden
it reveals stones of quartz

Es interminable
vuelve a comenzar

Interminable
it begins again

www.ingramcontent.com/pod-product-compliance
Lightning Source LLC
Chambersburg PA
CBHW070847160426
43192CB00012B/2346